NO LONGER PROPERTY OF
ANYTHINK LIBRARIES/
RANGEVIEW LIBRARY DISTRICT

JR. GRAPHIC MONSTER STORIES

SHAPE-SHIFTERS!

DAVID L. FERRELL

PowerKiDS
press.

New York

Published in 2014 by The Rosen Publishing Group, Inc.
29 East 21st Street, New York, NY 10010

Copyright © 2014 by The Rosen Publishing Group, Inc.

All rights reserved. No part of this book may be reproduced in any form without permission in writing from the publisher, except by a reviewer.

First Edition

Editor: Joanne Randolph
Book Design: Planman Technologies
Illustrations: Planman Technologies

Publisher Cataloging Data

Ferrell, David L.
Shape-shifters! / by David L. Ferrell.
p. cm. — (Jr. graphic monster stories)
Includes index.
ISBN 978-1-4777-6219-6 (library binding) — ISBN 978-1-4777-6220-2 (pbk.) — ISBN 978-1-4777-6221-9 (6-pack)
1. Werewolves — Juvenile literature. 2. Shapeshifting — Juvenile literature. I. Title.
GR830.W4 F47 2014
398.469—d23

Manufactured in the United States of America

CPSIA Compliance Information: Batch # W14PK1: For Further Information contact Rosen Publishing, New York, New York at 1-800-237-9932

Contents

Main Characters

Emily Isabella Burt (1841–1911) The subject of many werewolf stories focused around the area of Talbot County, Georgia.

Mildred Owen Burt (1812–1890) According to legend, responsible for the care of her daughter Emily, who was thought to be a werewolf.

Zeus King of the Greek gods. Could change his own shape and appearance to that of animals, other people, and objects. Could also cause others to change form.

Sigmund and Sinfjotl (ca. 1400s) Adventurers from Scandinavian mythology. Became trapped in wolf form after stealing and putting on wolf pelts belonging to skin-changers.

About Werewolves

- A **shape-shifter** is a person who can change from one thing into another. According to folklore, werewolves are humans who can change into wolves.

- According to legend, werewolves attack livestock and people, usually at night under a full moon. They can be very strong and difficult to kill.

- Some werewolves may have some wolflike features when they are in human form. These features include bushy eyebrows, hairy hands and faces, and sharp canine teeth. They may also have human features when in wolf form, such as humanlike eyes.

Shape-Shifters!

HOWL!

WOW! *WEREWOLF II* WAS AWESOME. WHAT DID YOU THINK, GABE?

I'M CONFUSED. WHY DIDN'T THE MAIN CHARACTER TURN INTO A WEREWOLF AFTER THE WEREWOLF BIT HIM?

ACTUALLY, THAT DOESN'T ALWAYS HAPPEN.

REALLY?

THAT'S RIGHT, ALAN. THERE'S A LOT OF WEREWOLF STUFF THAT HOLLYWOOD JUST MADE UP.

IT SOUNDS LIKE YOU KNOW A LOT ABOUT WEREWOLVES, NIRAJ. TELL US MORE.

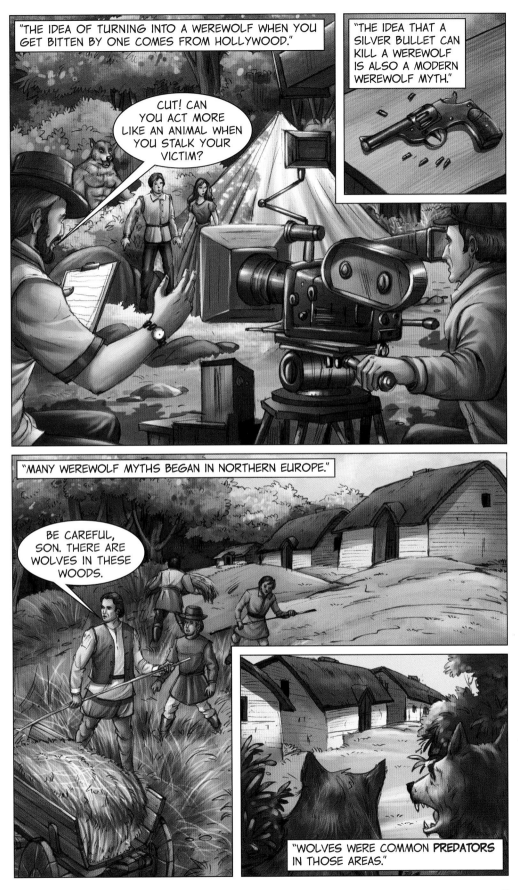

"SOME OF THE EARLIEST MYTHS ABOUT SHAPE CHANGERS COME FROM ANCIENT GREECE."

"IN ONE STORY, KING LYCAON TRIED TO TRICK THE GOD ZEUS INTO EATING HUMAN FLESH. ZEUS PUNISHED HIM BY TURNING HIM INTO A WOLF."

YOU WICKED MAN! YOU WILL SPEND THE REST OF YOUR LIFE AS A WOLF FOR YOUR EVIL DEEDS.

"A SIMILAR STORY, INVOLVING TWO HOLY MEN, APPEARS IN AN INDIAN LEGEND."

FRIGHTENING ME WITH THIS FALSE SNAKE WAS A DIRTY TRICK, SAHASRAPAT. I CURSE YOU TO BE A SNAKE!

"SHAPE CHANGING OFTEN CAME AS A CURSE OR FORM OF PUNISHMENT. IN NORSE TALES, THE DWARF FAFNIR AMASSED A GREAT TREASURE HOARD. BUT OVER TIME, HIS GREED TURNED HIM INTO A DRAGON."

"BUT THESE AREN'T THE ONLY EXAMPLES OF SHAPE CHANGERS. GODS AND GODDESSES COULD OFTEN CHANGE FORMS."

RUMBLE

MOO

"AT DIFFERENT TIMES, ZEUS TRANSFORMED HIMSELF INTO A BULL, A SWAN, A GOPHER, A CLOUD, AND A SHOWER OF GOLD COINS."

"THE BURTS WERE AN IMPORTANT FAMILY IN TALBOT COUNTY, GEORGIA. MILDRED OWEN BURT, A WIDOW AT AGE 37, HAD FOUR CHILDREN: SARAH, EMILY, MILDRED, AND JOEL."

"ACCORDING TO SOME TALES, EMILY, ONE OF THE DAUGHTERS, WAS A BIT ODD. SHE HAD BUSHY EYEBROWS AND LARGE CANINE TEETH."

"EMILY BURT WAS SAID TO BE A QUIET CHILD WHO KEPT TO HERSELF. SHE LOVED TO READ BOOKS ABOUT THE SUPERNATURAL."

"EMILY'S MOTHER FOUND HER DAUGHTER HUNTING IN A FIELD."

"SHE WAS FRIGHTENED BY HER DAUGHTER, WHO WAS CARRYING A CLEAVER."

"THINKING EMILY WAS A WEREWOLF, HER MOTHER FIRED AT HER."

EEEEK!

BOOM!

More Werewolf Stories

- **The Beast of Gévaudan**
  The beast of Gévaudan was a man-eating wolf that terrorized south-central France between 1764 and 1767. More than 240 attacks were reported with more than 100 people killed. The French army was brought in to kill the animal without success. As the attacks increased, they even caught the attention of King Louis XV. He sent in professional wolf hunters, including his personal rifle bearer. In September 1765, hunters killed a giant wolf in the area. Though the king declared victory, the attacks continued until June 1767. In that year, Jean Chastel, a local hunter, brought down another beast, and the attacks finally ended.

- **The Wolf of Ansbach**
  Attacks by a wolf were reported near Ansbach, Germany, in 1685. At first, the beast attacked only livestock, but soon it began stalking people as well. The townsfolk believed it was the spirit of their wicked mayor, who had recently died and returned in the form of a wolf. The people of Ansbach banded together and chased the wolf down an abandoned well, where they killed it. Then they took the body of the wolf, dressed it in human clothes to look like the mayor, and hung it in the middle of town.

- **The Beast of Bray Road**
  Many people have reported sightings of a strange beast along Bray Road near Elkhorn, Wisconsin. Witnesses describe a large doglike creature with brownish-gray fur, large teeth, and yellow eyes. Some report seeing it stand on its hind legs to a height of almost 7 feet (2 m). Not many people have suggested that it's a werewolf. However, those who have encountered it seem generally baffled by the creature.

Glossary

ascetic (uh-SEE-tik) Someone who lives very simply and eats very little for religious reasons.

berserkers (ber-SERK-erz) Ancient Scandinavian fighters who were said to be impossible to kill.

hoax (HOHKS) Something that has been faked.

invincible (in-VINT-suh-bel) Unable to be beaten.

lycanthropy (lih-KANT-thruh-pee) A person becoming a werewolf.

nagas (NAH-gahz) Serpent people of Indian legend.

paranormal (pa-ruh-NOR-mul) Not able to be explained by science.

penance (PEH-nunts) Doing something to show that one is sorry for something bad that one has done.

predators (PREH-duh-terz) Animals that kill other animals for food.

rational (RASH-nul) Having reason and understanding of the way things work.

shape-shifter (shape-SHIF-ter) A person with the ability to change his or her appearance, often changing into the form of an animal.

supernatural (soo-per-NA-chuh-rul) Having to do with a world that cannot be seen.

Index

Websites

Due to the changing nature of Internet links, PowerKids Press has developed an online list of websites related to the subject of this book. This site is updated regularly. Please use this link to access the list:

www.powerkidslinks.com/mons/shape